Stuart Barlow is a practising solicitor with over 40 years of experience in court litigation. He conducts most of his own advocacy and has dealt with many cases involving Litigants in Person. He has practised in the areas of Civil, Criminal and Family Law in South Wales and the East Midlands. He now specialises in Children Law. Stuart was a Chief Assessor of the Law Society Accreditation Scheme until 2016 and an Adjudicator for the Legal Aid Agency. He is also a former external examiner of the Nottingham Law School. He has written articles and presented courses on the subject of Litigants in Person over some years. He is also the author of two other law books.

A Practical Guide to Working With Litigants in Person and McKenzie Friends in Civil Proceedings

A Practical Guide to Working With Litigants in Person and McKenzie Friends in Civil Proceedings

Stuart Barlow
LLB (London) Solicitor

Law Brief Publishing

Published 2020 by Law Brief Publishing, an imprint of Law Brief Publishing Ltd
30 The Parks
Minehead
Somerset
TA24 8BT

www.lawbriefpublishing.com

Paperback: 978-1-913715-31-1

This book is dedicated to my three older brothers, John, Robert and Gordon, all of whom have been a source of encouragement to me over the years.

PREFACE

I have observed the workings of civil courts over many years. There have been significant changes in law and procedure during this time. Almost all of these changes have been positive and improved the way civil courts work.

One area that has been a challenge to courts and practitioners alike is the increase in the number of parties who attend court without legal representation. Many of these would have preferred to have instructed a lawyer but following the virtual abolition of legal aid in civil proceedings, have been unable to fund such representation. The end result is that civil courts deal with many cases with at least one unrepresented party. In cases where lawyers do represent a client and their opponent is a Litigant in Person, a particular approach to the case is called for on both sides. It is accepted that parts of the civil law procedure are better equipped to handle cases involving Litigants in Person. The Small Claims Court is designed with the Litigant in Person in mind. Other parts of the civil court system are complex where only experienced practitioners can navigate with confidence.

In writing this book, I have brought together materials from various sources to assist the lawyer especially, but also any Litigant in Person or McKenzie Friend who finds the content helpful.

The contents of the book as to law and procedure are correct as at 31st July 2020.

Stuart Barlow
July 2020

CONTENTS

INTRODUCTION

When I was training to be a solicitor, most towns in the country had a county court building. Bigger towns also had a district registry. Inside this building was at least one court room where a judge would sit to hear civil and family law cases. Close to the court room was an open plan area fronted by a long open counter with a small but efficient team of court staff administering the many court actions filed each day. If I was unsure about any court procedure or I was designated to issue civil court proceedings, I would walk round the corner to our local county court to seek out a court official who would put me on the right track. Those sitting behind that long counter seemed to take pleasure in helping the queue of people mesmerised by the abundance of court forms and documents in their hands. Many in the queue had no solicitor but were in need of help. From memory, the court staff treated everyone the same way and customer satisfaction appeared high. I expect that the assistance given at those court counters kept the judicial process running more efficiently than we can ever calculate.

Nowadays, many of those county courts have ceased to exist and with them the long public counters. Where the court building still remains open, security screens have now been erected and large signs make it clear that access to court staff is usually by appointment only. The existence of a Court Charter imposes limits on those accessing court procedures. Those practicing civil law are sufficiently conversant with the way the court system operates and can therefore cope with the changes. For many members of the public, however, civil courts have become inaccessible. They have no-one to ask the most basic of court questions. There is a group who seek to represent themselves in court known as Litigants in Person. Their number has grown enormously over the years and is seen in some court quarters as a problem. Litigants in Person choose to pursue their case without legal representation. This is their right. Efforts have been made to assist a Litigant in Person by producing a whole series of leaflets, guidance notes and booklets, some of which have been drawn up by government officials. To that extent, a Litigant in Person can feel well supported. Voluntary groups also give time and expertise to assist them. Despite this help being offered, a Litigant in Person can still feel disadvantaged within a court system which is, for the most part, designed for all parties to be legally represented. Even the small claims court takes some navigation. Some believe there is an inequality of arms leading to an unfairness in decision making. At the same time lawyers acting for a fee paying party are expected to conduct their client's case in a way that is professional, fair and just for all concerned, including an unrepresented opponent. The fee paying client may complain that the present court system favours the Litigant in Person simply because he has no legal representation. Costs, leniency in enforcing court orders and appeals are points in question. This book has been written to assist a lawyer instructed in a civil case where the opponent has no legal representation. The lawyer wants to bring about an outcome which balances his duty to the court, his duty to his paying client and his duty to the unrepresented opponent. This balancing act is not always easy to achieve, but constructive and practical advice is set out throughout the chapters of this book to assist in bringing about a satisfactory outcome.

CHAPTER ONE
LITIGANT IN PERSON (LIP)

1. Litigant in Person is the term which should be used in all criminal, civil and family courts to describe individuals who exercise their right to conduct legal proceedings on their own behalf.

2. The number of Litigants in Person has risen significantly in recent years and is likely to continue to do so as a result of financial constraints and the consequences of the Legal Aid reforms. Public funding in private proceedings is now available in only exceptional circumstances.

3. Litigants in Person are also appearing with increasing frequency in the Court of Appeal. Some have represented themselves at first instance. Others have had lawyers appear for them in the court below, take their own cases on appeal, sometimes as a result of withdrawal of public funding after the first instance hearing.

4. Those who exercise a personal right to conduct proceedings themselves, operate in what feels like an alien environment. All too often, the Litigant in Person is regarded as 'a problem' for Judges and for the Court system rather than a person for whom the system of Civil Justice exists (**Lord Woolf Access to Justice, Interim Report June 1995**).

5. The outcome of the case may have a profound effect and long-term consequences upon the life of a Litigant in Person. They may have agonised over whether the case was worth the

risk to their health and finances and, therefore, feel passion-
ately about their situation.

CHAPTER TWO
WHY IS THIS SEEN AS A
DIFFICULT SUBJECT?

1. It is curious that lay litigants have been regarded 'as problems', almost as nuisances for the Court system. This has meant that the focus has generally been upon the difficulties that Litigants in Person pose for the Courts rather than the other way round **(Professor John Baldwin Monitoring the Rise of the Small Claims Limit).**

2. **In 2013, a Judicial Working Party Chaired by Mr Justice Hickinbottom** summed up the position as follows:-

   "Providing access to Justice for Litigants in Person within the constraints of a system that has been developed on the basis that most Litigants will be legally represented, poses considerable and unique challenges for the Judiciary. Cases will, inevitably, take more time during a period of severe pressure on Judicial time. However, Litigants in Person are not in themselves "a problem"; the problem lies with a system which has not developed with a focus on unrepresented litigants. We consider it vital that, despite the enormous challenges presented, Judges are enabled and empowered to adapt the system to the needs of Litigants in Person, rather than vice versa".

3. A recent government report stated that judges estimate that cases involving a litigant in person can take 50% longer than those represented by a legal professional.

4. Ministry of Justice statistics for cases involving a Litigant in Person are in short supply but the figures we do have show,

without doubt, that the number of cases where both parties were represented has almost halved.

5.   There has been a dramatic change in recent times both in attitude and practice so the subject has become increasingly important, not only on the basis of what others have said, but perhaps more importantly, what practicing lawyers have experienced themselves. It is important that legal practitioners face up to these issues as they go to court each day.

CHAPTER THREE
WHY DO WE HAVE LITIGANTS
IN PERSON?

1. Many litigants in civil proceedings cannot afford to instruct a solicitor. This has been caused partly by the withdrawal of legal aid for many court applications, but also because of the level of fees charged by solicitors. Even fixed rates are beyond the scope of many parties.

2. Litigants may think that disputes can be easily agreed because the issue before the court appears to be quite straightforward. This may be the case; often it is not.

3. Some litigants believe that lawyers are only interested in making money and give a reason for their decision to represent themselves as a way out of filling legal pockets.

4. Certain Litigants feel they are more than capable of dealing with the matters themselves, whatever the complications. A Litigant in Person may prefer to present his/her case in a particular way or in a form that a qualified lawyer would not feel comfortable with. This may seem to be misguided, but a party to proceedings genuinely believes that given some research and asking a few friends the right questions, there is no need to involve anyone else. Some Litigants in Person will seek professional legal advice in advance of proceedings or a court hearing and then deal with the matter themselves

CHAPTER FOUR
FIRST POINT OF CONTACT WITH
A LITIGANT IN PERSON

Before a Hearing

The first point of contact with a Litigant in Person can be during the negotiations, in correspondence or on the telephone. It is good practice to inform or remind an unrepresented opponent that he/she is at liberty to seek help from a solicitor or other suitably qualified person at any time. There is likely to be a pre-action protocol in place for the claim in question which may bring a represented party in contact with the Litigant in Person.

At the hearing

This is the more common encounter when lawyers have their first face to face meeting with a Litigant in Person.

After the hearing

There may be a need to meet with a Litigant in Person to tie up some loose ends following a court hearing, possibly to sign some documents or to review the terms of an order made. It could be that a Litigant in Person has failed to turn up at a court hearing and there are a number of important matters still to be resolved. The court may have made an order in the absence of a Litigant in Person who now wants to challenge the terms of the order. Maybe the Litigant in Person has appealed against a court order made when he was legally represented but is now no longer legally represented.

CHAPTER FIVE
IMPLICATIONS OF WORKING WITH
A LITIGANT IN PERSON

1. Litigants in Person are not all the same

A lawyer should guard against thinking there is a stereotypical litigant. One must not think that all Litigants in Person will be difficult and awkward. That is not the case: many will be very cooperative and appreciate any help the lawyer can give them.

2. Costs can increase

In cases involving a Litigant in Person, there is frequently more work to be done by the lawyer acting for a legally represented party and the proceedings can be more costly for their client. More work is undertaken by the lawyer because a Litigant in Person has no experience in handling the work required. Sometimes a court order requires that the work is done by the represented party. For example, in the preparation of bundles for a court hearing. This may seem unfair on the represented party but there is often no way of avoiding it. Clients need to be made aware of this. The court may order the represented party to:

- Prepare all necessary bundles of documents and provide them to the court;

- Provide copies of bundles to a Litigant in Person at the same time as providing them to the court;

- Provide written arguments and documents to the court and to the Litigant in Person in good time before any hearing, unless a delay is unavoidable;

- Where necessary, promptly draw up and seal the order made by the court.

If these will give rise to significant expense to the represented party, the court should be asked either to direct the Litigant in Person to professional services [eg bundles] or to direct that the Litigant in Person bear the costs of the lawyer preparing the bundle.

3. Flexibility is required towards a Litigant in Person

Experience has shown that courts will often be more flexible towards a Litigant in Person. Judges will not be keen to admit this as they like to be seen to stick to the rules and deal with each party in the same way. Much of the case law supports this approach. However, experience shows that a judge is sometimes prepared to be more lenient towards a Litigant in Person, simply to have an effective hearing.

The court is obliged to afford procedural fairness to all parties, whether represented or appearing in person, and the duty of the court extends to providing appropriate assistance as required. Common Law and Article 6 compliance require:

- The right to be heard and the right to challenge evidence (a fair trial);

- Access to the same information and to production of the same documents;

- A person's right to know the case against them;

- The right to a decision affecting their rights;

- To be present and participate in hearings about the case;

- A reasoned decision.

The court may exercise these powers on application by one of the parties or of its own initiative. Achieving the overriding objective might require a judge to offer a degree of latitude towards a Litigant in Person whose preparation and presentation of case does not conform to the court rules, provided that this does not compromise due process. The effective management of a case involving a Litigant in Person might require more directions hearings than would otherwise be necessary.

4. The outcome of proceedings is less predictable

It is hard to predict certain success of any case but experience has shown that the outcome of a case involving a Litigant in Person is far less certain. Judges are under a duty to actively manage cases. This includes the freedom to extend or shorten the time for compliance with any rule, practice direction or court order; adjourn or bring forward a hearing; to receive evidence by phone or other means; decide the order in which issues are to be heard; exclude an issue from consideration; take any other step or make any other order for the purpose of managing the case and bringing about a fair hearing on both sides.

5. More contested hearings and appeals

In a case with a Litigant in Person, statistics show there are more contested hearings and more appeals. A compromise is so much harder without a lawyer on both sides. Sometimes a Litigant in Person may not appreciate that compromise is a vital part of court proceedings and is unclear how to achieve this. Some Litigants in Person would rather have their case heard and risk the outcome than settle a case on terms which are either uncertain or unknown. Appeals can be filed by a Litigant in Person on the basis there is nothing to lose.

In March 2018, Sir Terence Etherton identified that permission to appeal applications made by Litigants in Person in the civil division of the Court of Appeal stood at 42% of all applications for the 12 months ending 31 January 2018. Given that nearly half of all Court of Appeal matters now involve a Litigant in Person, it is important for both represented parties and a potential Litigant in Person to be aware of the latest developments concerning their treatment by the courts.

CHAPTER SIX
WHO ARE LITIGANTS IN PERSON?

1. There is no typical Litigant in Person. He/she may come from a diverse range of social and educational backgrounds. Some may be very skilled at representing themselves. A Litigant in Person's knowledge, aptitude and general attitude towards the proceedings are largely unknown quantities at the outset of the hearing.

2. The difficulties faced by a Litigant in Person often stem from their lack of knowledge of the law and court procedure. The procedure is so familiar to lawyers and judges that they often do not realise the extent of a Litigant in Person's misunderstanding. For many Litigants in Person, their perception of the court environment will be based on what they have seen on the television and in films. They can:-

    (i)   Be unfamiliar with the language and specialist vocabulary and legal proceedings;

    (ii)   Have little knowledge of the procedure involved, and find it difficult to apply the rules, even when they do read them up;

    (iii) Be ill-informed about ways of presenting evidence;

    (iv)   Be unskilled in advocacy, and so unable to undertake cross-examination or test the evidence of an opponent;

(v)   Be unable to understand the relevance of law and regulations to their own problem, or to know how to challenge a decision that they believe is wrong;

(vi) Lack objectivity and emotional distance from their case.

All these factors have an adverse effect on the preparation and presentation of their case.

How can lawyers help?

1. Lawyers can try to ensure that a Litigant in Person understands what is happening and what is expected of them at all stages of the proceedings – before, during and after any attendances at a hearing. This means that:-

    (i)   The process is explained to them in a manner that they can understand;

    (ii)   They have access to appropriate information (e.g. the Rules, Practice Directions and Guidelines] – whether from publications or websites;

    (iii) They are informed about what is expected of them in ample time for them to prepare or comply;

    (iv)   Whenever possible, they are given sufficient time for their particular needs;

2. Lawyers should try to maintain a balance between assisting and understanding what a Litigant in Person requires, while protecting the represented party against problems that can be

caused by a Litigant in Person's lack of legal and procedural knowledge.

3. Some Litigants in Person are unaware of the availability of explanatory leaflets at Court or the list of advice agencies. Citizens Advice Bureaux has an informative online information system, and individual bureaux may be able to offer assistance with case preparation. Whilst these possibilities should always be flagged up to a Litigant in Person, it is important not to overestimate the availability and extent of voluntary sector assistance. Advice agencies have been subject to severe cuts, both to grants and Legal Aid income in recent years. A Litigant in Person may have difficulty obtaining prompt appointments or finding the level of specialist expertise needed. The experience of trying to find help without success can itself, be very demoralising.

4. Some Litigants in Person believe that Court staff are there to give legal advice. Under the Courts' Charter, Court staff can only give information on how a case may be pursued; they cannot give legal advice under any circumstances. The lawyer may have to explain this to a Litigant in Person. This problem can be made more difficult by the restrictions placed on accessibility of court counters.

CHAPTER SEVEN
UNDERSTANDING THE
DIFFICULTIES

Language

English (or Welsh) may not be the first language of a Litigant in Person, and he/she may have particular difficulties with the written language. Any papers received from the court or from the other party may need to be translated. In some circumstances, an interpreter will be required.

Disability

A Litigants in Person with mental or learning disabilities may have difficulty in presenting their case and giving evidence. Difficulties faced by disabled witnesses are likely to be exacerbated where the individual is representing him or herself.

A Litigant in Person may be a vulnerable adult and require additional support from the court or the lawyer. If a Litigant in Person is vulnerable and their needs have not been recognised, a legal representative should bring this to the court's attention, as they would for a client. This also applies when the legal representative has doubts about an opponent's capacity to conduct court proceedings.

Applications, Statements, and Time Limits

Litigants in Person may make basic errors in the preparation of a civil case by:-

(i)   failing to choose the best course of action or response;

(ii) failing to put the important points in their application or statement;

(iii) describing their case clearly in non-legal terms, but failing to apply the correct legal label or any legal label at all;

(iv) overlooking time limits and not understanding the relevant law and evidence required for an application to extend time;

(v)   A Litigant in Person can think that acceptance of his/her application form and processing of the documents means that the correct procedure has been adopted. The litigant can therefore be taken by surprise when, at a later stage, he/she has to deal with this issue;

(vi) where directions are given in writing, a Litigant in Person may not understand exactly what he/she is supposed to do, or may not have the skillset to do it correctly.

Case Preparation

A Litigant in Person may not know:-

(i)   Where to send information and documents and in what format. An instruction such as "Send it to the Defendant by (date)" can cause uncertainty;

(ii)   Who is "the Defendant"? The Litigant in Person may be uncertain whether this means sending to the Defendant personally or their Solicitor or Barrister or whether the court has to be copied in.

(iii) If sending it to the court is sufficient?

(iv)   If e-mail is allowed?

(v)   If documents can be scanned and sent?

Short Deadlines for Directions or Orders

A Litigant in Person can sometimes take longer to carry out tasks than represented parties because of the unfamiliarity with the process and uncertainty of what to do. They may also be receiving advice from a Citizens Advice Bureau or other source, and may have to wait for an appointment.

Pressure from Represented Party

Sometimes a represented party can add to a sense of confusion and overload by sending repeated letters demanding more information and threatening to go back to court for orders or costs orders. It may, or may not be legitimate for a represented party to be taking this approach. A Litigant in Person can be frustrating and even uncooperative and can make it very hard for the other side to understand and prepare the case for hearing. Careful thought should be given to bring about the most appropriate and fair result.

Compliance with Directions or Orders

A Litigant in Person may not realise that court orders are more than aspirational. He or she may also fail to understand that if he or she does not comply with an order, he or she is at risk of an application being dismissed or a costs order being made against him or her. Although letters advising of the consequences of non-compliance are sent, a Litigant in Person may not understand the formal words and jargon involved. *For example, non-compliance, unless order etc.*

Having said this, cases do need to be prepared and the other side is entitled to a level of information and co-operation from a Litigant in Person.

Disclosure of Documents

The duty to disclose documents is sometimes neglected by a Litigant in Person.

(i) Some may have little or no appreciation that they should adopt a "cards on the table" approach and will try to hold back key documents until the hearing.

(ii) Some may hold back text messages, emails etc.

(iii) A Litigant in Person may not understand what documents count as *relevant*. They may need to be told, for example, that diaries and text message exchanges are included;

(iv) Late disclosure of relevant documents can cause delays at a hearing and can lead to an adjournment.

Trial Bundles

The term *Court bundle* can cause confusion. It should be explained that this simply means a tagged or lever arch file of documents. A Litigant in Person may find it difficult to understand the difference between disclosure and collating documents for the trial bundle. It needs to be explained to him/her that not all documents which have been disclosed need to be seen by the court at the final hearing.

CPR 39.5 requires a claimant to file bundles unless the court orders otherwise. Where the claimant is a Litigant in Person the court will often order that the represented party prepares and files the bundle. The represented party will need to agree the content of the bundle with the Litigant in Person and a record kept as to what efforts are made to arrive at an agreement on this subject. The court may permit the Litigant in Person to file an additional bundle if the Litigant in Person believes material documents have been omitted.

Statements of Case and Witness Statements

A statement of case must be concise and comply with CPR 16 and be structured clearly to enable a response to be produced. The same rules apply to Litigants in Person as they do to represented parties. It may be the court will allow more leeway to a Litigant in Person than to those who have professional lawyers. Where a Litigant in Person files an inadequate statement of case legal representatives can apply to strike out and or apply for summary judgement. Alternatively, an application for further information under **CPR 18**. In practice, the court is likely to exercise its discretion and offer some leniency to a Litigant in Person who files an inadequate statement of case by affording them the opportunity to rectify the position. An offer by the represented party to the Litigant in Person to do this voluntarily by specific dates may assist both sides and save costs.

Litigants in Person sometimes do not realise they will have to give evidence themselves at a court hearing. They may not know what a witness statement is and their role in giving evidence at a hearing. A Litigant in Person should be informed of the consequences of failing to file or serve his or her own witness statement in advance of the hearing. A Litigant in Person may not understand that a witness statement is of little value without attendance of the witness in support. He or she should be directed to the witness templates available from the court office or online.

Adjournments

Litigants in Person may not appreciate that they need permission of the court for an adjournment if a hearing date presents them with difficulties. A Litigant in Person may also fail to think about the fact that the other party may incur costs if the adjournment request is made right at the last moment. A Litigant in Person might ask for an adjournment or an extension of time in circumstances where the lawyer believes this is unnecessary. For example, a Litigant in Person might genuinely not appreciate the importance of the attendance of witnesses.

The granting of an adjournment or extension is always a matter of discretion and courts may more readily grant an application when it is sought by a Litigant in Person. The appellate courts are particularly concerned to ensure that a Litigant in Person is given every opportunity to present his/her case, in so far as that is consistent with fairness. A judge is more likely to grant an adjournment or extension where a submission or issue catches a Litigant in Person by surprise.

Sources of Law

Most Litigants in Person do not have access to legal textbooks or libraries where such textbooks are available and may not be able to download information from a legal website. Sometimes Litigant in Person do not understand the role of Case Law and are confused by the fact that the Judge appears to be referring to someone else's case.

Compromise

A Litigant in Person can face potential difficulties in relation to compromise and negotiated settlements. He or she may not realise it is possible or how to go about it procedurally. He or she may not have had access to advice on the merits or value of his/her claim and may not know how to go about negotiation. He/she may not even realise that they are allowed to speak to the other side with a view to trying to reach a compromise. A judge's approval is required for any consent order where one party is a Litigant in Person, and the consent order must be signed by the Litigant in Person CPR 40.6(2)(b) and CPR 40.6 (7)(c) It is good practice to insert in the consent order that the Litigant in Person has been advised to take independent legal advice. This can avoid later arguments over the Litigant in Person challenging the content of the consent order.

The Real Issues of the Case

A Litigant in Person may not appreciate the real issues in the case. It is vital to identify and, if possible, establish agreement as to the issues to be tried so that all parties proceed on this basis. Time spent in this way can shorten the length of proceedings considerably.

Advocacy

A Litigant in Person can have difficulty in understanding that because there is a version of events being presented that is different from their own, this does not necessarily mean that the other side is being untruthful. A Litigant in Person may not understand the importance of "putting" his or her key points to the other side's witnesses. Terms like "submissions" and "speech" may be unfamiliar. Advocates are expected to draw to the court's attention a fair picture of the law and not omit cases which go against his or her side's interests. The judge may take on the role of asking questions to ensure the Litigant in Person has a fair hearing. This may need to be explained to the represented party by his/her legal representative.

How can a Lawyer help?

1. The lawyer should try to give a clear explanation to a Litigant in Person of what the court is being asked to order and the reasons for such request. Try to use peoples' names rather than labels such as Claimant or Defendant.

2. Lawyers find it relatively easy to précis and identify key points of an argument. For many other people this is extremely difficult. As a result, when ordered to provide information, a Litigant in Person can either miss the

deadline, avoid the task altogether or do it wrongly. If template or standard forms are available, the lawyer can direct a Litigant in Person to where they can be accessed together with any available guidance notes.

3. Where practical, a lawyer should avoid asking for orders that a Litigant in Person will find confusing or difficult to deal with. Ordering a Litigant in Person to provide complex responses is rarely a good idea. Where necessary, it may be better to hold a directions hearing and talk a Litigant in Person through the case, extracting the required information and recording them in the court order and thus overseen by the court.

4. As far as possible, the lawyer should seek to set deadlines that take into account the reasonable needs and resources of both parties. Excessively short deadlines should be avoided. Where a court order is being discussed at court, the lawyer can ask a Litigant in Person how long he or she needs to comply with a court order, impressing upon him or her the importance of sticking to their estimate.

CHAPTER EIGHT
COSTS AND LITIGANTS
IN PERSON

Litigants in Person (Costs and Expenses) Act 1975 (as amended) gives a Litigant in Person the right to recover sums in respect of any work done, and any expenses and losses incurred, by a litigant in or in connection with the proceedings to which the order relates.

This Act applies all civil and family courts and establishes the principle that a costs order can be made against a represented party. The mechanics of how this works in practice are found in the **Civil Procedure Rules**

Under **rule 46.5 of the Civil Procedure Rules** the court may award a litigant in person their costs.

Whilst neither the 1975 Act nor the Civil Procedure Rules (CPR) defines a Litigant in Person, **CPR 46.5(6)** states that a Litigant in Person can include a company or other corporation, a barrister, a solicitor, a solicitor's employee, a manager of a body recognised under **section 9 of the Administration of Justice Act** 1985 (incorporated practices) and a person who, for the purposes of the **Legal Services Act 2007**, is authorised to conduct litigation.

This means that a person who acts on his own behalf for either all or part of the claim is likely to be a Litigant in Person, unless represented. However, the fact that legal representation may be for only part of the proceedings does not preclude a successful Litigant in Person from recovering costs for the aspect of work he conducted while not represented – **Agassi v Robinson (HM Inspector of Taxes) [2005] EWCA Civ 1507**.

Rule 46.5 is set out in full below:

(1) This rule applies where the court orders (whether by summary assessment or detailed assessment) that the costs of a litigant in person are to be paid by any other person.

(2) The costs allowed under this rule will not exceed, except in the case of a disbursement, two-thirds of the amount which would have been allowed if the litigant in person had been represented by a legal representative.

(3) The litigant in person shall be allowed –

(a) costs for the same categories of –

(i) work; and

(ii) disbursements,

which would have been allowed if the work had been done or the disbursements had been made by a legal representative on the litigant in person's behalf;

(b) the payments reasonably made by the litigant in person for legal services relating to the conduct of the proceedings; and

(c) the costs of obtaining expert assistance in assessing the costs claim.

(4) The amount of costs to be allowed to the litigant in person for any item of work claimed will be –

(a) where the litigant can prove financial loss, the amount that the litigant can prove to have been lost for time reasonably spent on doing the work; or

(b) where the litigant cannot prove financial loss, an amount for the time reasonably spent on doing the work at the rate set out in Practice Direction 46.

(5) A litigant who is allowed costs for attending at court to conduct the case is not entitled to a witness allowance in respect of such attendance in addition to those costs.

(6) For the purposes of this rule, a litigant in person includes –

(a) a company or other corporation which is acting without a legal representative; and

(b) any of the following who acts in person (except where any such person is represented by a firm in which that person is a partner) –

(i) a barrister;

(ii) a solicitor;

(iii) a solicitor's employee;

(iv) a manager of a body recognised under section 9 of the Administration of Justice Act 1985; or

(v) a person who, for the purposes of the 2007 Act, is an authorised person in relation to an activity which constitutes the conduct of litigation (within the meaning of that Act).

A Litigant in Person seeking to claim costs may present a claim calculated in one of two ways:

(a)   An hourly rate to reflect actual financial loss, or

(b)   where unable or unwilling to establish actual loss, on a fixed hourly charge.

The hourly charge is currently £19.

In respect of either category, the maximum a Litigant in Person can recover for time is two-thirds of the amount that would have been allowed if legally represented. This limit does not apply to disbursements.

In respect of financial loss, it is for a Litigant in Person to establish by evidence and on the balance of probability that a financial loss has been suffered and the amount involved. Where a loss is shown, a Litigant in Person may recover that loss, even if the loss is less than the flat rate of £19 per hour.

If a Litigant in Person has not suffered a financial loss, or is unable to show a financial loss, then the flat rate applies.

Whether a Litigant in Person shows a financial loss, claims at the flat rate, or a mixture of the two, the figure allowed in total (excluding disbursements) cannot exceed two-thirds of the amount that would have been allowed if legally represented.

If a Litigant in Person seeks costs, either of an interim application, or trial, the Litigant in Person should file and serve written evidence to show actual loss at least 24 hours prior to any hearing.

A successful Litigant in Person who obtains an order for costs may recover:

a) Costs for the same categories of:

    i. Work; and

    ii. Disbursements, which would have been allowed if the work had been done or the disbursements had been made by a legal representative on the Litigant in Person's behalf;

b) The payments reasonably made by the Litigant in Person for legal services relating to the conduct of the proceedings; and

c) The costs of obtaining expert assistance in assessing the costs claimed. **CPR 46.5(3)**.

In respect of **CPR 46.5(3)(c)** 'expert assistance' is defined in **PD 46 para 3.1** as assistance from a barrister, solicitor, fellow of the Chartered Institute of Legal Executives, Fellow of the Association of Costs Lawyers, or a Law Costs Draftsman who is a member of the Academy of Experts or the Expert Witness Institute.

For 'work done', it has to be work that a legal representative would have undertaken, or a disbursement that would have been paid on a Litigant in Person's behalf.

In **Agassi** the costs of employing a tax expert to undertake litigation work were not recoverable as a disbursement since a legal representative would not have employed a third party to undertake such work.

If no loss can be shown, then the figure is an amount in respect of time reasonably spent. See **rule 45.39(5)**.

Court decisions

When making an award in favour of a Litigant in Person, the Court should:

a) Identify a rate, being either the actual loss, or the prescribed rate of (say) £19;

b) Assess the time reasonably/necessarily/proportionately spent;

c) Assess the figure a hypothetical legal adviser of an appropriate grade would have charged for the same work;

d) Allow either the Litigant in Person's assessed claim in full, or, if necessary, discount the figure to two-thirds of the amount that would have been charged by the legal representative; and

e) Assess the disbursements.

Courts have sympathised with unrepresented parties as they are not being represented by a trained lawyer. However, in *Veluppillai v Veluppillai* **[2015] EWHC 3095 (Fam)** a costs order was made against an unrepresented party.

Cost orders can be awarded against a party if they fail to adhere to Court directions, make unwarranted applications, or generally conduct themselves in an unreasonable manner.

In **Veluppillai** the wife was claiming for financial remedy following divorce, the conduct of the husband was described as 'abysmal' and led to over 30 hearings over a 3-year period. The husband had made threats to kill against the wife and her barrister for which he was committed to prison for contempt. He had been repeatedly warned by judges about his unpleasant menacing conduct in court. On one occasion he assaulted the wife and her barrister in court for which he was later convicted of assault. He skipped his sentencing hearing and fled overseas from where he bombarded the court with abusive emails claiming that he had a fatal illness and demanding that the proceedings be adjourned indefinitely. The Judge found favour with the wife's position and made an Order in the terms sought by her and ordered that the husband should pay the wife's costs assessed in the sum of £146,609.

CHAPTER NINE
RULES OF ENGAGEMENT

Rules and Practice in Litigant in Person cases

This chapter discusses the relationship between a lawyer's duty to the client, the duty to the court and the administration of justice, and the extent to which the latter duty requires a lawyer to assist a Litigant in Person. There have always been Litigants in Person in the courts and in principle an increase in their number should not of itself have any bearing on a lawyer's professional duties towards the court or the client. The increase in Litigants in Person does, however, have practical implications for the way matters are conducted.

The professional and regulatory framework

A lawyer's paramount duty is to the court and to the administration of justice. **The Legal Services Act 2007 s1(3)** *referring to lawyers as 'authorised persons', provides that…authorised persons should act in the best interests of their client,*

> *(d) …persons who exercise before any court a right of audience, or conduct litigation in relation to proceedings in any court, by virtue of being authorised persons should comply with their duty to the court to act with independence in the interests of justice…'*

> *That duty may operate to the potential disadvantage of a lawyer's client by, for example, requiring that the lawyer should not mislead the court or withhold from it, documents and authorities even when they detract from the client's case. Subject to that, a lawyer's duty is to their client.*

Bar Standards Board

Every barrister is bound by the core duties in the Bar Standards Board Handbook (the 'BSB Handbook'). The guidance at **gC1** identifies when particular duties may take precedence over others. This includes the statement at **gC1.1** that the duty to the court in the administration of justice overrides any other core duty, if and to the extent that the two are inconsistent.

> **Rule C3 states:** *You owe a duty to the court to act with independence in the interests of justice. This duty overrides any inconsistent obligations which you may have (other than obligations under the criminal law).*
>
> *It includes the following specific obligations which apply whether the barrister is acting as an advocate or is otherwise involved in the conduct of litigation in whatever role (with the exception of rule C3.1 below, which applies when acting as an advocate):*
>
> - *you must not knowingly or recklessly mislead or attempt to mislead the court;*
>
> - *you must not abuse your role as an advocate;*
>
> - *you must take reasonable steps to avoid wasting the court's time;*
>
> - *you must take reasonable steps to ensure that the court has before it, all relevant decisions and legislative provisions; and*
>
> - *you must ensure that your ability to act independently is not compromised.*

Rule C4 states: *'Your duty to act in the best interests of each client is subject to your duty to the court'.*

The BSB Handbook also makes this specific reference to Litigant in Person: 'gC5 Your duty under rule C3.3 includes drawing to the attention of the court any decision or provision which may be adverse to the interests of your client. It is particularly important where you are appearing against a litigant who is not legally represented'.

If a barrister is contacted directly by a Litigant in Person, the barrister's clerk or the barrister himself should let the Litigant in Person know whether it is appropriate for the Litigant in Person to speak with the barrister or the solicitor.

Barristers must still exercise their professional independence about this issue and have regard to the best interests of their client. For example, if the purpose of the discussion is related to the conduct of the litigation, referral to the instructing solicitor (or the client in a public access case) would be appropriate. If the communication is related to the barrister's role as advocate, the barrister would be entitled to refer the communication to the solicitor (or client), but it may be appropriate for the barrister to communicate with the Litigant in Person directly, particularly if the issues are matters that ordinarily would be discussed between barristers.

Chartered Institute of Legal Executives Regulation

The Chartered Institute of Legal Executives **Regulation Code of Conduct** applies to their members, practitioners and Authorised Entities.

It provides that they must:

> '1. Uphold the rule of law and the impartial administration of justice:
>
> 1.1 Understand and comply with your primary and overriding duty to the court, obey court orders and do nothing which would place you in contempt.
>
> 1.2 Not knowingly or recklessly allow the court to be misled.
>
> 2.2 Not engage in any conduct that could undermine or affect adversely the confidence and trust placed in you and your profession by your client, your employer, professional colleagues, the public and others'.

Rule 4 of the CILEx Rights of Audience Conduct Rules provides: *'CILEx advocates have a primary and an overriding duty to the court to ensure in the public interest, that the proper and efficient administration of justice is achieved. They must assist the court in the administration of justice and must not deceive the court or knowingly or recklessly mislead it'*.

Rule 5 provides that: *'CILEx advocates must not engage in conduct, whether in the exercise of their rights of audience or otherwise, which is:*

> a) *dishonest or otherwise discreditable to an advocate;*
>
> b) *prejudicial to the administration of justice; or*
>
> c) *likely to diminish public confidence in the legal profession or the administration of justice, or otherwise bring the legal profession into disrepute'*.

Solicitors Regulation Authority

Chapter 5 of the Solicitors Regulation Authority Handbook:

'Your client and the court', includes the following provisions:

- *'Outcome (5.1) you do not attempt to deceive or knowingly or recklessly mislead the court;*

- *Outcome (5.5) where relevant, clients are informed of the circumstances in which your duties to the court outweigh your obligations to your client;*

- *Outcome (5.6) you comply with your duties to the court.'*

The SRA Handbook covers relations with third parties at chapter 11: 'This chapter is about ensuring you do not take unfair advantage of those you deal with and that you act in a manner which promotes the proper operation of the legal system'.

- *Outcome 11.1 - you do not take unfair advantage of third parties in either your professional or personal capacity;*

- *Indicative Behaviour 11.7 - you do not take unfair advantage of an opposing party's lack of legal knowledge where they have not instructed a lawyer.*

- *Taking 'unfair advantage' refers to behaviour that any reasonable lawyer would regard as wrong and improper. That might include:*

- *bullying and unjustifiable threats;*

- *misleading or deceitful behaviour;*

- *claiming what cannot be properly be claimed; or*

- *demanding what cannot properly be demanded.*

Solicitors client care obligations under the SRA Handbook apply as much to 'unbundled' services as they do to a full retainer.

Knowing and using law and procedure effectively against your opponent because you have the skills to do so, whether that be against a qualified representative or a Litigant in Person, is not taking 'unfair advantage' or a breach of any regulatory code.

Summary

- There is a paramount duty to the court and the administration of justice.

- That duty to the court will take precedence if it conflicts with a duty to a client.

- If the duty to the court outweighs an obligation to the client.

- A lawyer must not take unfair advantage of a Litigant in Person.

- There is no obligation to help a Litigant in Person to run their case or to take any action on a Litigant in Person's behalf. By doing so the lawyer might be failing in his duties to his own client – *Khudados v Hayden [2007] EWCA Civ 1316@ paragraph 38.*

A Litigant in Person's written case may be unclear. It is not part of a lawyer's role to re-write the case for the Litigant in Person. There are obvious advantages in attempting to ensure that the essential issues are clear. A lawyer could invite the court to identify the issues, which helps to make clear to the Litigant in Person that it is only those issues that should be addressed. The judge could at the same time explain what evidence is admissible. If a legal representative is required to give assistance to a Litigant in Person, the reasons for this should be explained to the client. Unless otherwise ordered by the court, or to further the legal representative's duty to the court, assistance should not be given a Litigant in Person if there is a cost to the client and the legal representative's client is not prepared to meet the cost.

CHAPTER TEN
MCKENZIE FRIENDS

The term 'McKenzie Friend' refers to an individual who assists a Litigant in Person in presenting the case in a court room by taking notes, quietly making suggestions or giving advice. The role differs from that of an advocate in that the McKenzie Friend does not address the court or examine any witnesses. A person may not be permitted to perform the role of McKenzie Friend if unsuitable, eg someone who is pursuing their own or an unsuitable agenda. Individuals may also wish for their McKenzie Friend to act as their advocate. This also requires the court's permission as with any other lay person seeking rights of audience.

How did it begin?

In 1970 Mrs McKenzie was divorcing Mr McKenzie. She was legally represented at the contested divorce hearing. Mr McKenzie was unrepresented. He did, however, have the help of an Australian barrister who attended court with Mr McKenzie but did not have the right to act as his advocate as he had no right of audience in an English court.

The barrister had hoped to assist Mr McKenzie by taking notes and giving quiet advice during the hearing. The judge asked the barrister to leave the court and sit in the public gallery, leaving Mr McKenzie with no help at all. The case went against Mr McKenzie who then appealed to the Court of Appeal. The Court of Appeal ruled that he had been deprived of the assistance to which he was entitled, and ordered a retrial. This case created Mc Kenzie Friends.

Much has been written about McKenzie Friends over the last few years and has become a growth area in cases involving Litigants in Person.

Guidance as to the circumstances in which a McKenzie Friend can be involved in civil and family proceedings can be found in the **Practice Guidance (McKenzie Friends: Civil and Family Courts)** issued by the Master of the Rolls and the President of the Family Division on 12th July 2010.

The full text is set out in the Addendum at the end of this book.

McKenzie Friends are intended to help and a lawyer should work on this basis. They are not substitute lawyers. They are there to support rather than represent a Litigant in Person.

The 2010 Practice Guidance is not a Practice Direction and does not have the same force of authority, but courts will, in practice, usually follow it routinely. Legal representatives need to be familiar with this document and be clear as to what a McKenzie Friend can and cannot do. Some McKenzie Friends, especially those who act in this role on a regular basis, know the guidance well. Lawyers need to be prepared to argue their case on any restrictions, if necessary.

Judges usually appreciate help in making decisions on the involvement of a McKenzie Friend. Advocates play an important role in these circumstances.

McKenzie Friends are **allowed** to:

Provide moral support for the litigant, take notes, help with case papers and quietly give advice on the conduct of the case.

McKenzie Friends are **not allowed** to:

Act as a litigants' agent in relation to the proceedings, manage the litigants case out of court, for example by signing court documents or address the Court make oral submissions or examine witnesses. These restrictions can be varied by permission of the court to do so.

Note, however, that **Sections 27 & 28 Court and Legal Services Act 1990** make it clear what it means to have rights of audience and the right to conduct litigation. These sections give the Court discretionary powers to grant individuals lay rights. The Court may grant an unqualified person a Right of Audience, in exceptional circumstance only, and only on very careful consideration.

A Litigant in Person must apply at the outset of the hearing if he or she wishes a McKenzie Friend to be granted a Right of Audience or Right to Conduct Litigation.

Legal representatives have a right to object to the involvement of a McKenzie Friend and any applications made to exercise additional rights. Courts will usually follow the suggestions set out in the Practice Guidance to lean in favour of allowing a McKenzie Friend to be present in court to assist a Litigant in Person. A court will be more cautious in allowing additional rights.

It should be emphasised that a McKenzie Friend cannot attend a court hearing unless the Litigant in Person has received permission from the court.

There is a **Form of Application** to become a McKenzie Friend available at court. Court ushers will usually have these available on request. This form should be used by the Litigant in Person in all cases. Legal Representatives may wish to stress the importance of completing this form before going into court.

A copy of this Form of Application can be found in the Appendix at the end of this book.

When the role of McKenzie Friends came into being, those involved were usually a friend or colleague. However, in more recent years the position of the McKenzie Friend has, in some instances changed. A professional McKenzie Friend has come into being. Individuals now offer themselves to a Litigant in Person as an alternative to a qualified lawyer. They advertise their services as professional McKenzie Friends on a fee-paying basis. These fees are often much lower than a qualified lawyer. Whilst some McKenzie Friends may belong to a professional organisation, many act as individuals. Other than the **Practice Guidance 12th July 2010** there is no formal regulation of their role nor are there any court rules specifically governing their activities. Such services are available nationwide and are very active in certain parts of the country.

An Ongoing Debate

There is some ongoing debate about the role and functions of the McKenzie Friend. **The Lord Chief Justice and Judicial Board** has issued a **Consultation** specially focusing on the McKenzie friend. Despite the Consultation having been set up as far back as February 2017, no final conclusions have been reached.

The Consultation has been seeking views on a number of issues including:

1. Whether the term "McKenzie Friend" is appropriate and if there is a more suitable alternative;

2. Whether McKenzie Friends should be paid;

3. Whether the court rules should be amended to regulate the activities of McKenzie Friends;

4. Courts in Scotland already have rules governing their equivalent of the McKenzie Friend, and these are referred to in the Consultation document.

5. The Consultation document also raises additional matters such as the need to for a plain language guide to assist a Litigant in Person as well as fee recovery.

6. Whilst changes are likely, nothing is certain in view of the competing interests of the professional and consumer groups, who have made their views known within the consultation and broadly support the work of the McKenzie Friend.

CHAPTER ELEVEN
PARTICULAR HELP FOR A
LITIGANT IN PERSON

Support Through Court

Support Through Court (previously The Personal Support Unit) is available in certain courts round the country. These courts offer help to unrepresented parties (a Litigant in Person) involved in civil and family proceedings. Often, the larger the court, the more likely there is such help for the unrepresented party. Support Through Court is a charity staffed largely by volunteers. They cannot give legal advice as they are not legally trained but they can offer practical and emotional support to people facing a court without a lawyer, including help with completing the court forms. Information can be provided as to where legal advice can be found. The volunteer can accompany the Litigant in Person whilst in court but cannot speak on their behalf. The service is free of charge.

Barrister Direct Access

Anyone can now go directly to a barrister, for advice and/or representation, without having to involve anyone else. Barristers can advise a Litigant in Person on their legal status and rights. Barristers can draft and send documents for the Litigant in Person and represent him/her in court. The main advantage of the Direct Access Scheme for consumers of legal services is the opportunity to save on legal costs, specifically solicitor's fees. However, removing solicitors from the process of running a legal case often requires that clients themselves must perform the majority of document management, filing, and other related activities in the context of conducting litigation. Barristers are not allowed to take on direct access clients unless doing so is in both the client's best interests and in the interests of justice. In complicated cases, barristers must recommend to clients that they obtain external support from a solicitor. However, since the expense of using a solicitor can potentially defeat the cost-saving purpose of the Direct Access Scheme, consumers have the option of using a provider of **Public Access Legal Support Service (PALS)**, which is a specialised paralegal resource catering to barristers and clients who work together within the framework of the Direct Access Scheme. This service is, of course, available to a Litigant in Person in civil proceedings.

CHAPTER TWELVE
CASE LAW

Recent civil decisions show that a Litigant in Person is not able to blame non-compliance with important legal provisions merely on their unrepresented status.

An important decision underlining this point is **Barton v Wright Hassall LLP [2018] UKSC 12.**

In this case, a Litigant in Person issued a claim form and elected to serve this on the defendant himself. On the last day prior to the deadline for service of the claim form, the claimant emailed the defendant's solicitors, attaching the claim form by way of service. However, he had not obtained permission from them to serve the claim form electronically, and he was subsequently informed that as they had not indicated that they would accept service by email, the claim form had expired and the action was now statute-barred. The claimant made an application for an order validating service retrospectively, and this proceeded to the highest appellate court.

The Supreme Court found that, although in the current climate of cuts to legal aid, acting as a Litigant in Person was not always by choice, "it will not usually justify applying to litigants in person a lower standard of compliance with rules or orders of the court".

The Civil Procedure Rules provide a framework within which to balance the interests of both sides, and if a Litigant in Person was entitled to greater indulgence in complying with these rules then this would affect that balance. Unless the rules in question were "particularly inaccessible or obscure", a Litigant in Person should familiarise himself with any relevant rules which apply. The rules in this instance were not inaccessible or obscure, and so the claimant's appeal was dismissed.

The Supreme Court also stated that although the defendant's solicitors could have warned the claimant that they did not accept service by email, they were under no duty to do so.

Similarly, in **Reynard v Fox [2018] EWHC 443 (Ch)**, the claimant argued that because he was a Litigant in Person, it would be unjust for his claim to be struck out because it had not been brought under the correct provision, as he did not have a detailed knowledge of insolvency regulations. However the judge determined that none of the rules in question were "hard to find, difficult to understand or … ambiguous", and the claimant was an intelligent litigant who had learned a great deal about insolvency law and procedure. Accordingly, no injustice arose merely due to the claimant's status as a Litigant in Person.

The position was further considered in **EDF Energy Customers Ltd v Re-Energized Ltd [2018] EWHC 652 (Ch)**, in which the defendant company's director appeared on its behalf.

In considering whether a Litigant in Person should have been allowed to adduce arguments at a hearing of a winding-up petition which he had already made during an application for an injunction which had been dismissed, the judge emphasised that the Litigant in Person was not the only party to consider, and that delays and lack of finality impacted on the represented party and the courts as well. It would not be right to allow a party to act in person at first instance, and if the result went against them, to allow them to appeal with legal representation and present the same arguments again, or arguments which could have been made but which were not.

The judge derived the following principles from existing case law:

1. *There is a general duty on courts to assist litigants, depending on the circumstances, but it is for the court to decide what this duty requires in any particular case and how best to fulfil it, whilst remaining impartial.*

2. *The fact that a litigant is acting in person is not in itself a reason to disapply procedural rules or orders or directions, or excuse non-compliance with them.*

3. *The granting of a special indulgence to a litigant in person may be justified where a rule is hard to find or it is difficult to understand, or it is ambiguous.*

4. *There may be some leeway given to a litigant in person at the margins when the court is considering relief from sanctions or promptness in applying to set aside an order.*

Accordingly, it appears that a Litigant in Person will only be able to rely on the fact that he is a Litigant in Person in limited circumstances. Represented parties should be mindful of the level of assistance that they are expected to provide to assist the Court and their opponent when they are working with a Litigant in Person.

Summary of Cases involving Litigants in Person

No special treatment by the court

Tinkler v Elliott (2012) EWCA Civ 1289

The self-representing Mr Elliott failed to attend a hearing but instead submitted a medical certificate of unfitness to attend court. The High Court set aside the judgement holding that Mr Elliott had a good reason for not attending the original hearing. The Court of Appeal restored the original court's decision holding that the court rules need to be rigorously applied and that there were no special rules for a Litigant in Person.

Jones v Longley & Others (2015) EWHC 3362 (Ch)

The court said that a Litigant in Person is not subject to any special rules and are is as liable as represented litigants to have costs orders made against them.

Barton v Wright Hassall LLP (2018) UKSC Civ 12

The Supreme Court decided that the civil procedure rules would not be applied differently to unrepresented litigants. While the court could offer leeway in how litigants were handled during case management hearings or during the trial, this would not usually justify applying a lower standard of compliance with rules or orders of the court. The court also indicated that solicitors should not be expected to flag up procedural mistakes made by a Litigant in Person on the other side.

Failure to comply with Directions

Hobson v West London Law Solicitors (2013) EWHC 4425 QB

A High Court decision to strike out a claim as a result of the failure by the claimant, a Litigant in Person, to comply with the rules and court orders, where the claimant's inaction had serious implications for the litigation process and the defendant.

Timely Disclosure

Re B (Litigants in Person: Timely Service of Documents) (2017) EWHC 2365 (Fam)

The court reminded legal practitioners of the need to adapt normal practices when dealing with a Litigant in Person. Minimum service requirements should be adapted in individual cases to protect the rights of a Litigant in Person and may be necessary to prevent the intrinsic unfairness to a Litigant in Person that may arise from late service.

This judgment, published with the approval of the President of the Family Division, arose from a final hearing in a child abduction case in which legal documents comprising counsel's position statement (14 pages) and four law reports (100 pages) were given at the door of the court to a non-English-speaking litigant in person. Whilst Mr Justice Peter Jackson acknowledges that the position statement was of real assistance to the court, time was wasted before the hearing whilst the mother studied the documents with the help of the court-appointed interpreter.

Mr Justice Peter Jackson reminded advocates of the obligations imposed by **Practice Direction 27A** concerning court bundles and, in particular, paragraph 6. He noted that paragraph 6 sets out the minimum service requirements and that they should be adapted in individual cases to protect the rights of a Litigant in Person in order to prevent the intrinsic unfairness to a Litigant in Person that may arise from late service.

Duty to the court

East of England Ambulance NHS Trust v Sanders [2014] UKEAT/ 0217/14/RN at [48]-[51]

This judgment is a reminder of three points of wider application:

(1) *that lawyers must ensure that they comply with the rules and practice directions, and be aware that a failure to do so which affects a Litigant in Person – whether or not the court is also affected – may lead to adverse consequences for the lawyer or the lawyer's client;*

(2) *that lawyers should be seeking to identify practical steps that might be taken, in the interests of both the court and their own client, to assist the smoother running of a case or a hearing, including through assisting the Litigant in Person to follow what is going on and to understand the points of law to be made, and then to take any such steps as can be taken without undue cost or adverse impact on their own clients; and*

(3) *that there will often by a 'duty to the court' basis for taking a particular course which benefits a Litigant in Person.*

Court procedure when a Litigant in Person involved

In the case of **Agarwala v Agarwala [2016] EWCA Civ. 1252 at paragraph [72]** Lady Justice King stated:

"Whilst every judge is sympathetic to the challenges faced by litigants in person, justice simply cannot be done through a torrent of informal, unfocussed emails, often sent directly to the judge and not to the other parties. Neither the judge nor the court staff can, or should, be expected to field communications of this type. In my view judges must be entitled, as part of their general case management powers, to put in place, where they feel it to be appropriate, strict directions regulating communications with the court and litigants should understand that failure to comply with such directions will mean that communications that they choose to send, notwithstanding those directions, will be neither responded to nor acted upon."

McKenzie Friends

LFA v LSL (2017) EWFC B62

In a family matter the husband applied for his McKenzie Friend to be granted rights of audience. This was opposed by the wife arguing that the Guidance on McKenzie Friends advised that the court should be slow to grant any application from a Litigant in Person for a right of audience or a right to conduct litigation to a lay person, including a McKenzie Friend. The court refused the husband's application but allowed the McKenzie Friend to remain in court to provide quiet advice to the husband. The McKenzie Friend became increasingly disruptive during the hearing. The judge took the unusual step of excluding the McKenzie Friend from the court room for the remainder of the hearing.

CHAPTER THIRTEEN
WHILST AT COURT

1. Meeting with a Litigant in Person.

If a case gets to a court hearing, careful thought should be given on how the lawyer will relate to his/her unrepresented opponent. Beyond the usual introductions, what are the particular topics and issues he or she intends to discuss with a litigant?

The lawyer should try to work out an action plan in advance. Time will be limited at the hearing so an informal agenda could be helpful to any discussions. Thought should be given as to where in the court building discussions will take place which will save embarrassment and preserve confidentiality. This is as important to a Litigant in Person as it is to a represented client. If an interview room is not available (and these are at a premium in most courts) then a suitable alternative meeting place needs to be found. A crowded waiting area should be avoided. A lawyer should remember to explain to his client why a meeting with a Litigant in Person is necessary and what will be discussed. This is important to ensure that a client is confident his/her case is not being compromised. Some advocates prefer to have the meeting with a Litigant in Person in the presence of a colleague. In any event, it is good practice to make a note of any material explanation or assistance given to a Litigant in Person.

2. Give more court time than usual.

Lawyers should not arrive at court a few minutes in advance of the hearing expecting everything to go well. It is important to arrive in good time to meet and greet a Litigant in Person. This gives an opportunity of getting to know an opponent better and have adequate time for discussions. The lawyer should set aside enough time in the office diary to give to the case. A Litigant in Person will not understand the need for a lawyer to get away from court to deal with other matters back at the office or attend another court hearing. Out of respect for a Litigant in Person, a lawyer should never double book a court hearing. It will almost certainly create unnecessary stress to those concerned, inconvenience the court and reduce the chance of an agreement.

3. Explain to an opponent, in advance, what the Court is being asked to decide on.

Advocates should not spring surprises. The court will not be impressed if this happens. A failure to give advance notice can delay the court hearing. It is not unknown for a court to put a case back to a time later in the day to give a Litigant in Person time to consider matters before the court. If a Litigant in Person is the claimant in the case, the lawyer for the defendant could offer to introduce the case to the court. This gesture can send out a positive message to a Litigant in Person and appreciated by the parties and the court.

4. Explain to an opponent how the hearing works and who can go into Court.

The lawyer should keep this simple and answer any queries a Litigant in Person has regarding the hearing itself. A Litigant in Person may expect to take a friend or supporter into court as of right. Explain that permission from the court is required for others to go into the court hearing. If a Litigant in Person is requesting a McKenzie Friend to assist him or her, explain how this is addressed and where the necessary form of application can be found. A lawyer may need to discuss this request with his client before deciding on whether any objections should be put forward to the court.

5. Encourage unrepresented opponents to engage with an opponent.

This sounds like commonsense but it is surprising how many advocates are reluctant to engage with the opposite side. A Litigant in Person may refuse to do so. Occasionally, he/she may be rude or aggressive, but this is likely to be a very rare occurrence. Lawyers should take care to avoid using language that might confuse, including the use of abbreviated terms or legal jargon. A Litigant in Person may resent the case being conducted in a way that means he or she cannot understand what is happening. A lawyer should go out of his way to explain the court process in a way that a Litigant in Person will understand and point them in the direction of information he/she will find useful. The court will expect an advocate to have made efforts to discuss issues before going into court.

6. Avoid being combative.

This is not always easy especially with a difficult opponent. Being combative only irritates and sometimes can anger an opposing party.

7. Take copies of important documents to Court.

Litigants in Person may fail to bring their own copy documents to court, not realising the need to do so. Handing over a further copy can be helpful to all concerned and appreciated by an unrepresented opponent. It can save time and inconvenience.

8. Check what documents have been filed at Court.

Check with a Litigant in Person first and with the Court after that. That way a lawyer will not be taken by surprise when a judge points out that a Litigant in Person has filed a bundle of documents, none of which has seen by the advocate or even been made aware of. Simple checks can save time and embarrassment.

9. Encourage the represented client to be flexible and open minded.

A lawyer can expect a judge to explain to a Litigant in Person how the hearing will proceed, such as the order of calling witnesses and the right which he or she has to cross-examine a witness. An advantage of these explanations being given in court is that they take place in front of the client. If a client asks why the court is apparently going out of its way to help a Litigant in Person, a lawyer can explain that it is in the interests of fairness and justice and ultimately in your client's interest for the judge to do so. This is not easy for a client to understand in these circumstances. Most clients are there to win, not to concede. Not an easy message to convey to a client.

10. Explain the lawyers' responsibilities to a client.

It is important a client appreciates why a lawyer is giving some assistance to an opposing party. It should be emphasised that a lawyer has a professional duty to the court and that in the interests of fairness, a lawyer may be required to provide procedural assistance to a Litigant in Person. There are potential benefits for a client in assisting a Litigant in Person. This could include avoiding time taken at hearings, delays through adjournments and the associated costs to a client in terms of their money and time. A lawyer should not give assistance to a Litigant in Person if it involves a cost to a client who is not willing to meet that cost. If a lawyer believes that a request from the court to provide assistance to a Litigant in Person goes beyond a duty to the court or places a lawyer in a conflict with a duty to a client, the lawyer should draw this to the attention of the court and invite the judge to reconsider.

CHAPTER FOURTEEN
SPECIFIC SUBJECTS IN THE
COURT PROCESS

Correspondence

1. Legal representatives should adopt a professional, co-operative and courteous approach at all times.

2. Correspondence should be carefully considered for its potential effect on a Litigant in Person. Any communications should aim to resolve issues and settle matters, not antagonise or inflame them.

3. Email correspondence should be handled with care as it is not a secure medium. It is also important to take care, if asked to communicate by fax or email, that the recipient is aware, agrees and can receive faxes or emails in a confidential environment. The first contact with a Litigant in Person might well set the tone for the way in which the case is dealt with from then on. An initial letter should briefly address the issues. Avoid protracted, clearly one-sided and unnecessary arguments or assertions. The legal representative should consider asking the Litigant in Person their preferred method of correspondence at the outset. If provided, this will assist in proving to the court that correspondence has been brought to the attention of the Litigant in Person in accordance with their preference. The formal requirements for service under **CPR 6** should, however, always be complied with.

4. In an initial contact, and at other suitable stages in any dispute, a lawyer should recommend to a Litigant in Person

that he seeks independent legal advice, or point them to other advice or support agencies. A failure to do so may result in the court allowing the Litigant in Person additional time or adjournment or opportunity to seek a wasted costs order.

5. Legal representatives should consider providing the website address for HMCTS Handbook for Litigants in Person.

6. Care should be taken to communicate clearly and to avoid any technical language or legal jargon. Any legal jargon should be explained where it cannot be avoided.

7. Responding promptly to correspondence and telephone calls will help a client's case and also in relating to a Litigant in Person. Correspondence and telephone calls from a Litigant in Person may occasionally be emotive, repetitive, and potentially hostile. This does not mean that a lawyer has to tolerate unacceptable behaviour nor does it mean that a Litigant in Person has a right to expect a lawyer to respond immediately to his/her calls or correspondence.

8. Legal representatives should send a copy of any relevant pre-action protocol to the Litigant in Person.

Injunctions

In actions involving an injunction or similar application, it is essential that allegations of behaviour are treated seriously, but it is also important for the lawyer to remain objective and to allow for the possibility that they may be untrue or exaggerated.

After advice, a lawyer may be instructed to write to an opponent to record the incident, demand cessation of the actions and indicate that further action might or will be taken if it does not cease. Some say that letters demanding cessation are threatening and raise the temperature, so it is important to be sure that such a statement is justified in the circumstances.

Lawyers should think carefully about how they can present the issues to an opponent. If costs are an issue, a client may be willing to forego a claim for costs if an agreement is reached. The court may be involved at some stage in the process, but some early planning as to an approach could help all concerned.

Exploring with a Litigant in Person the difference between a Court Order and an Undertaking to the Court is not an easy task. A lawyer may have to leave such matters to the court to handle, especially if an opponent is unwilling or unsure about discussing these matters.

In any event, if a lawyer arrives at an agreed position with a Litigant in Person, the terms and consequences of such agreement should be explained by the court and recorded in the Court Order.

Small Claims

Parties on the small claims track often act in person (Litigant in Person) and so the case management provisions have been focused and designed to make the dispute resolution process as quick, cheap and straightforward as possible. The court has a very wide discretion as to the conduct of the proceedings. Many parts of the CPR do not apply to small claims and recoverable costs are very limited. Hearings will usually be heard before a District Judge who can grant the same types of remedies as though the case were proceeding on the fast track or multi track. The Small Claims Court will usually give standard directions and fix a date for the trial without the need for the parties to attend a case management conference. The court will tend to limit cross examination and the judge will opt to question the witnesses themselves where possible. Whilst the hearings are in public, they tend to be informal, usually taking place in the judge's room, rather than a court room. The court can adopt any procedure it believes to be fair and appropriate to the dispute. Generally, the strict evidence rules don't apply: evidence does not need to be on oath and the court can limit cross examination. Parties to a small claim track can be represented at the hearing by a lawyer or a lay representative (**CPR PD 27 para 3.2(2)**). Alternatively, they can represent themselves. Parties are obliged to consider alternative dispute resolution (ADR) at all stages of the litigation process. While there are different forms of ADR on the small claims track, a small claims mediation service has been established to encourage parties to participate in mediation.

The Small Claims Mediation Service is a free and confidential service for court users involved in the small claims cases which have been defended. To participate in the service, all parties must agree to enter mediation in good faith with the aim of achieving settlement. Mediation appointments are usually carried out by telephone although face to face appointments can be made. After parties have filed directions questionnaires, and where a mediation is to take place, the court office will be in contact with the parties to arrange a mediation appointment. If mediation is unsuccessful, the case will be listed for a small claims hearing. As mediation is confidential, the judge will not be informed of anything said during the mediation.

The **Lay Representatives [Rights of Audience] Order 1999 (and CPR 27 PD 3.2 (2))** authorises lay representatives to appear in small claims. It provides that a lay representative may not exercise any right of audience (1) where the party fails to attend the hearing, (2) at any stage after judgment, or (3) on any appeal. The court has discretion to hear a lay representative even in any of these circumstances but granting a right to appear in an excluded case would require reasons. A lay representative exercising this right may be restricted if he or she is unruly, misleads the court or demonstrates unsuitability.

Rights of audience – Litigants in Person and Lay Representatives

Rights of audience are governed by **Part 3 of the Legal Services Act 2007 which came into force on 1 January 2010.** The current position is that where the Litigant in Person wishes a lay person to conduct the litigation, or act as their advocate, different issues arise. Under that Act, both rights are restricted to professional lawyers whose professional body authorises them to act as advocates. Other than Litigants in Person themselves (who are the subject of a specific exemption), lay persons can neither conduct litigation nor act as advocates for Litigants in Person; nor has a Litigant in Person any right to receive such assistance or to authorise such a lay person to act in such a way under a power of attorney. The courts have adopted a cautious approach to allowing lay assistants to be advocates in any case, although they have in practice been more flexible since the advent of the CPR.

Generally, the practice has been that where it will be beneficial to the fair and just determination of a case to have a lay person conduct a hearing on behalf of a Litigant in Person, then the right is granted in the interests of justice.

The following is helpful guidance to the court on whether to grant a lay person the right to speak as set out in the judgment of Mr Justice Hickinbottom in **Graham v Eltham Conservative & Unionist Club and Ors [2013] EWHC 979 (QB):**

In exercising the discretion to grant a lay person the right of audience, the authorities stress the need for the courts to respect the will of Parliament, which is that, ordinarily, leaving aside Litigants in Person who have a right to represent themselves, advocates will be restricted to those who are subject to the statutory scheme of regulation.

***Section 1(1) of the 2007 Act** sets out a series of 'statutory objectives' which includes ensuring that those conducting advocacy adhere to various 'professional principles', maintained by the rigours of the regulatory scheme for which the Act provides, and without which it is considered lay individuals should not ordinarily be allowed to be advocates for others. The strength of this interest and will is enforced by (i) legislative provisions allowing lay representation in types of claim in which such representation is considered appropriate, eg in small claims in the county court and (ii) the fact that to do any act in purported exercise of a right of audience when none has been conferred is both a contempt of court and a criminal offence.*

Consequently, it has been said by the higher courts that 'the discretion to grant rights of audience to individuals who did not meet the stringent requirements of the Act should only be exercised in exceptional circumstances', and, in particular, 'the courts should pause long before granting rights to individuals who [make] a practice of seeking to represent otherwise unrepresented litigants'

In line with the overriding objective of dealing with cases justly **(CPR Rule 1.1)**, the court will be more open to exercising its discretion and granting a right of audience in a particular case when it is persuaded it will be of assistance to the case as a whole if a litigant in person were to have someone who is not an authorised advocate to speak for him or her. That will especially be so if the litigant in person is vulnerable, unacquainted with legal proceedings or suffering from particular anxiety about the case he or she is conducting.

As a result, courts have in practice become more flexible about allowing litigants in person to have assistance at a hearing. In particular, they do not infrequently allow a relative or friend to speak on a party's behalf. Often, that relative or friend is well-attuned to the party's case and wishes, and puts the matter more articulately and coherently than the party could himself or herself.

As a result, the hearing can become more focused, more efficient and shorter. Such flexibility has become more important as the result of legal aid reforms (including those in the Legal Aid, Sentencing and Punishment of Offenders Act 2012, effective from 1 April 2013), which have resulted in a very substantial reduction in those entitled to public assistance and hence a substantial increase in litigants in person who now appear before the courts.

However, even though the legal world has in many ways moved on since the time of the authorities to which I have referred, in my view, as those authorities and the Practice Guidance stress, due deference to the will of Parliament, and general caution, are still required.

Therefore, as required by the Practice Guidance (paragraph 24), without undue formality, when a Litigant in Person wishes to be heard by way of a lay advocate, he should make an appropriate application to the court at the first inter partes hearing. The application should be made by the Litigant in Person, and not by the person who he or she wishes to be the advocate: although, often, in practice that other person may in fact be heard on the application. The application should be inter partes, to enable any opponent who may have objections to raise them. Generally, once the right to appear as an advocate has been given to lay person, that right will extend to all hearings in that claim, unless specifically directed otherwise or the right is revoked. The court may always revoke the right, any decision to revoke being informed by the same principles that apply to the grant of the right. It may, for example, be appropriate to revoke the right if, contrary to hopes and expectations, the lay advocate proves unhelpful or even positively disruptive.

Pre-action protocols in Civil Litigation

The aim of a pre-action protocol is to ensure that all reasonable steps have been taken to avoid the necessity of litigation. A pre-action protocol outlines specific procedures to be followed before issuing proceedings. The protocols do not amend any statutory time limit that apply. A practice direction on pre-action conduct of cases forms part of the Civil Procedure Rules. The aim of the protocols is to:

- allow cases to be dealt with as quickly, justly and cheaply as possible;

- ensure both parties have access to the documents and information they need at an early stage;

- encourage the use of alternative dispute resolution (ADR), such as mediation and arbitration;

- allow appropriate offers to resolve the issue to be made.

Only certain claims are subject to pre-action protocols. Where a pre-action protocol applies, the parties involved in the case are expected to follow it.

Current pre-action protocols include:

- personal injury;

- resolution of clinical disputes;

- construction and engineering;

- defamation;

- professional negligence;

- judicial review;

- disease and illness;

- housing disrepair;

- possession claims by social landlords;

- possession claims for mortgage arrears;

- dilapidation of commercial property;

- low value personal injury road traffic accident claims;

- low value personal injury (employers' liability and public liability) claims.

Where no pre-action protocol applies, the parties are expected to follow the Practice Direction on Pre-Action Conduct. This means parties are expected to act reasonably in exchanging information about the claim, defences and counter-claim, including relevant documents in support of their case. They should also consider the suitability of mediation or another form or ADR to resolve the issues.

The court will expect parties to have complied with any pre-action protocol applicable to their claim. The court can consider compliance when making any order for costs and/or giving case management directions. For example, the court can reduce the costs to be awarded to the successful party or order that the party at fault pay the costs of the proceedings.

CHAPTER FIFTEEN
WHERE DO WE GO
FROM HERE?

There is no real sign that the position of a Litigant in Person is likely to change, certainly in the foreseeable future. Looking at the statistics and comments of the judiciary and other legal commentators, the Litigant in Person is here to stay.

Assuming this is correct, it important that lawyers train up for their role in working with a Litigant in Person. Preparation will repay many times over. It is proposed that:

1. Lawyers become familiar with their professional rules regarding their role in working with a Litigant in Person.

2. Lawyers should forewarn their client at an early stage as to how working with a Litigant in Person affects him or her. Manage their expectations from the beginning.

3. Lawyers should think carefully about where the boundaries are drawn between their duty to the Court, their duty to their client; and a working relationship with an unrepresented opponent.

CHAPTER SIXTEEN
USEFUL INFORMATION

There are numerous sources of information available generally to people who wish to represent themselves. Set out below are details of helpful publications for both Litigants in Person and lawyers alike and a number of useful links to various organisations.

Gov.uk – Represent Yourself in Court
A government information website providing information across a range of subjects, including how to represent yourself in family legal matters and at court. The site includes links to downloadable forms.
https://www.gov.uk/represent-yourself-in-court

Ministry of Justice – Forms
Ministry of Justice (MoJ) downloadable forms and guidance.
https://www.gov.uk/government/collections/court-and-tribunal-forms

Advice Now
Advice Now is an independent advice organisation. Its website includes downloadable guidance covering a range of issues. It also provides information about legal aid.
https://www.advicenow.org.uk

Advice Guide
Advice Guide is the information and advice website of the Citizens Advice Bureaux (CAB). You can find information about the legal issues relating to divorce and separation as well as your local CAB.
https://www.citizensadvice.org.uk

Support Through Court (previously Personal Support Unit)
Support Through Court provide practical and emotional help and
support to people representing themselves at court. At present, they
are available in eight major court centres; go to the website for
further information about locations and services.

Civil Mediation Council
A charity which aims to promote the resolution of disputes by the
use of mediation. Information about mediation, Mediation Information and Assessment Meetings (MIAMs) and a directory of
mediators.
https://civilmediation.org   07841 01790

Money Advice Service
Advice and information about dealing with financial matters.
https://www.moneyadviceservice.org.uk

Publications

- Litigants in Person: Guidelines for Lawyers June 2015

  The Law Society, in conjunction with the Bar and the
  Institute of Chartered Legal Executives, has produced a very
  full document called "Litigants in Person Guidelines for
  Lawyers June 2015" which, you will find quite a useful document. Most of the contents still stand, despite the fact that
  the document goes back some years. At the end of this publi-
  cation that there are a couple of guidance notes specially
  drafted to assist the Litigant in Person and your client.

- A Handbook for Litigants in Person – Courts & Tribunals
  Judiciary (December 2012) written by various High Court
  judges.

- The Interim Applications Court of the Queen's Bench Division of the High Court – A guide for Litigants in Person (revised April 2013).

- The Bar Council's A Guide to Representing Yourself in Court (April 2013).

- A guide to proceedings in the Supreme Court for those without a legal representative (February 2014).

- *The Law Society's Litigants in Person: Guidelines for Lawyers (June 2015)*

- House of Commons Briefing Paper (2016) *Litigants in Person: the rise of the self-represented litigant in civil and family cases*

APPENDIX A
PRACTICE GUIDANCE:
MCKENZIE FRIENDS
(CIVIL AND FAMILY COURTS)

Practice Guidance: McKenzie Friends (Civil and Family Courts) dated the 12 July 2010 still stands as current authority.

Source: https://www.judiciary.uk/wp-content/uploads/JCO/Documents/Guidance/mckenzie-friends-practice-guidance-july-2010.pdf

1) This Guidance applies to civil and family proceedings in the Court of Appeal (Civil Division), the High Court of Justice, the County Courts and the Family Proceedings Court in the Magistrates' Courts.[1] It is issued as guidance (**not** as a Practice Direction) by the Master of the Rolls, as Head of Civil Justice, and the President of the Family Division, as Head of Family Justice. It is intended to remind courts and litigants of the principles set out in the authorities and supersedes the guidance contained in *Practice Note (Family Courts: McKenzie Friends) (No 2)* [2008] 1 WLR 2757,

---

1 References to the judge or court should be read where proceedings are taking place under the Family Proceedings Courts (Matrimonial Proceedings etc) Rules 1991, as a reference to a justices' clerk or assistant justices' clerk who is specifically authorised by a justices' clerk to exercise the functions of the court at the relevant hearing. Where they are taking place under the Family Proceedings Courts (Childrens Act 1989) Rules 1991 they should be read consistently with the provisions of those Rules, specifically rule 16A(5A).

which is now withdrawn.[2] It is issued in light of the increase in litigants-in-person (litigants) in all levels of the civil and family courts.

The Right to Reasonable Assistance

2) Litigants have the right to have reasonable assistance from a layperson, sometimes called a McKenzie Friend (MF). Litigants assisted by MFs remain litigants-in-person. MFs have no independent right to provide assistance. They have no right to act as advocates or to carry out the conduct of litigation.

What McKenzie Friends may do

3) MFs may: i) provide moral support for litigants; ii) take notes; iii) help with case papers; iii) quietly give advice on any aspect of the conduct of the case.

What McKenzie Friends may not do

4) MFs may not: i) act as the litigants' agent in relation to the proceedings; ii) manage litigants' cases outside court, for example by signing court documents; or iii) address the court, make oral submissions or examine witnesses.

---

2 *R v Leicester City Justices, ex parte Barrow* [1991] 260, *Chauhan v Chauhan* [1997] FCR 206, *R v Bow County Court, ex parte Pelling* [1999] 1 WLR 1807, *Attorney-General v Purvis* [2003] EWHC 3190 (Admin), *Clarkson v Gilbert* [2000] CP Rep 58, *United Building and Plumbing Contractors v Kajla* [2002] EWCA Civ 628, *Re O (Children) (Hearing in Private: Assistance)* [2005] 3 WLR 1191, *Westland Helicopters Ltd v Sheikh Salah Al-Hejailan (No 2)* [2004] 2 Lloyd's Rep 535. *Agassi v Robinson (Inspector of Taxes) (No 2)* [2006] 1 WLR 2126, *Re N (A Child) (McKenzie Friend: Rights of Audience) Practice Note* [2008] 1 WLR 2743.

Exercising the Right to Reasonable Assistance

5) While litigants ordinarily have a right to receive reasonable assistance from MFs the court retains the power to refuse to permit such assistance. The court may do so where it is satisfied that, in that case, the interests of justice and fairness do not require the litigant to receive such assistance.

6) A litigant who wishes to exercise this right should inform the judge as soon as possible indicating who the MF will be. The proposed MF should produce a short curriculum vitae or other statement setting out relevant experience, confirming that he or she has no interest in the case and understands the MF's role and the duty of confidentiality.

7) If the court considers that there might be grounds for circumscribing the right to receive such assistance, or a party objects to the presence of, or assistance given by a MF, it is not for the litigant to justify the exercise of the right. It is for the court or the objecting party to provide sufficient reasons why the litigant should not receive such assistance.

8) When considering whether to circumscribe the right to assistance or refuse a MF permission to attend the right to a fair trial is engaged. The matter should be considered carefully. The litigant should be given a reasonable opportunity to argue the point. The proposed MF should not be excluded from that hearing and should normally be allowed to help the litigant.

9) Where proceedings are in *closed court*, i.e.the hearing is in chambers, is in private, or the proceedings relate to a child, the litigant is required to justify the MF's presence in court. The presumption in favour of permitting a MF to attend such hearings,

and thereby enable litigants to exercise the right to assistance, is a strong one.

10) The court may refuse to allow a litigant to exercise the right to receive assistance at the start of a hearing. The court can also circumscribe the right during the course of a hearing. It may be refused at the start of a hearing or later circumscribed where the court forms the view that a MF may give, has given, or is giving, assistance which impedes the efficient administration of justice. However, the court should also consider whether a firm and unequivocal warning to the litigant and/or MF might suffice in the first instance.

11) A decision by the court not to curtail assistance from a MF should be regarded as final, save on the ground of subsequent misconduct by the MF or on the ground that the MF's continuing presence will impede the efficient administration of justice. In such event the court should give a short judgment setting out the reasons why it has curtailed the right to assistance. Litigants may appeal such decisions. MFs have no standing to do so.

12) The following factors should not be taken to justify the court refusing to permit a litigant receiving such assistance:

(i) The case or application is simple or straightforward, or is, for instance, a directions or case management hearing;

(ii) The litigant appears capable of conducting the case without assistance;

(iii) The litigant is unrepresented through choice;

(iv) The other party is not represented;

(v) The proposed MF belongs to an organisation that promotes a particular cause;

(vi) The proceedings are confidential and the court papers contain sensitive information relating to a family's affairs

13) A litigant may be denied the assistance of a MF because its provision might undermine or has undermined the efficient administration of justice. Examples of circumstances where this might arise are: i) the assistance is being provided for an improper purpose; ii) the assistance is unreasonable in nature or degree; iii) the MF is subject to a civil proceedings order or a civil restraint order; iv) the MF is using the litigant as a puppet; v) the MF is directly or indirectly conducting the litigation; vi) the court is not satisfied that the MF fully understands the duty of confidentiality.

14) Where a litigant is receiving assistance from a MF in care proceedings, the court should consider the MF's attendance at any advocates' meetings directed by the court, and, with regard to cases commenced after 1.4.08, consider directions in accordance with paragraph 13.2 of the Practice Direction Guide to Case Management in Public Law Proceedings.

15) Litigants are permitted to communicate any information, including filed evidence, relating to the proceedings to MFs for the purpose of obtaining advice or assistance in relation to the proceedings.

16) Legal representatives should ensure that documents are served on litigants in good time to enable them to seek assistance regarding their content from MFs in advance of any hearing or advocates' meeting.

17) The High Court can, under its inherent jurisdiction, impose a civil restraint order on MFs who repeatedly act in ways that undermine the efficient administration of justice.

Rights of audience and rights to conduct litigation

18) MFs do **not** have a right of audience or a right to conduct litigation. It is a criminal offence to exercise rights of audience or to conduct litigation unless properly qualified and authorised to do so by an appropriate regulatory body or, in the case of an otherwise unqualified or unauthorised individual (i.e., a lay individual including a MF), the court grants such rights on a case-by-case basis.[3]

19) Courts should be slow to grant any application from a litigant for a right of audience or a right to conduct litigation to any lay person, including a MF. This is because a person exercising such rights must ordinarily be properly trained, be under professional discipline (including an obligation to insure against liability for negligence) and be subject to an overriding duty to the court. These requirements are necessary for the protection of all parties to litigation and are essential to the proper administration of justice.

20) Any application for a right of audience or a right to conduct litigation to be granted to any lay person should therefore be considered very carefully. The court should only be prepared to grant such rights where there is good reason to do so taking into account all the circumstances of the case, which are likely to vary greatly. Such grants should not be extended to lay persons automatically or without due consideration. They should not be granted for mere convenience.

---

3 Legal Services Act 2007 s12 – 19 and Schedule 3.

21) Examples of the type of special circumstances which have been held to justify the grant of a right of audience to a lay person, including a MF, are: i) that person is a close relative of the litigant; ii) health problems preclude the litigant from addressing the court, or conducting litigation, and the litigant cannot afford to pay for a qualified legal representative; iii) the litigant is relatively inarticulate and prompting by that person may unnecessarily prolong the proceedings.

22) It is for the litigant to persuade the court that the circumstances of the case are such that it is in the interests of justice for the court to grant a lay person a right of audience or a right to conduct litigation.

23) The grant of a right of audience or a right to conduct litigation to lay persons who hold themselves out as professional advocates or professional MFs or who seek to exercise such rights on a regular basis, whether for reward or not, will however **only** be granted in exceptional circumstances. To do otherwise would tend to subvert the will of Parliament.

24) If a litigant wants a lay person to be granted a right of audience, an application must be made at the start of the hearing. If a right to conduct litigation is sought such an application must be made at the earliest possible time and must be made, in any event, before the lay person does anything which amounts to the conduct of litigation. It is for litigants to persuade the court, on a case-by-case basis, that the grant of such rights is justified.

25) Rights of audience and the right to conduct litigation are separate rights. The grant of one right to a lay person does not mean that a grant of the other right has been made. If both rights are sought their grant must be applied for individually and justified separately.

26) Having granted either a right of audience or a right to conduct litigation, the court has the power to remove either right. The grant of such rights in one set of proceedings cannot be relied on as a precedent supporting their grant in future proceedings.

Remuneration

27) Litigants can enter into lawful agreements to pay fees to MFs for the provision of reasonable assistance in court or out of court by, for instance, carrying out clerical or mechanical activities, such as photocopying documents, preparing bundles, delivering documents to opposing parties or the court, or the provision of legal advice in connection with court proceedings. Such fees cannot be lawfully recovered from the opposing party.

28) Fees said to be incurred by MFs for carrying out the conduct of litigation, where the court has not granted such a right, cannot lawfully be recovered from either the litigant for whom they carry out such work or the opposing party.

29) Fees said to be incurred by MFs for carrying out the conduct of litigation after the court has granted such a right are in principle recoverable from the litigant for whom the work is carried out. Such fees cannot be lawfully recovered from the opposing party.

30) Fees said to be incurred by MFs for exercising a right of audience following the grant of such a right by the court are in principle recoverable from the litigant on whose behalf the right is exercised. Such fees are also recoverable, in principle, from the opposing party as a recoverable disbursement: CPR 48.6(2) and 48(6)(3)(ii).

Personal Support Unit & Citizen's Advice Bureau

31) Litigants should also be aware of the services provided by local Personal Support Units and Citizens' Advice Bureaux. The PSU at the Royal Courts of Justice in London can be contacted on 020 7947 7701, by email at rcj@thepsu.org.uk, their website: www.thepsu.org.uk or at the enquiry desk. The CAB at the Royal Courts of Justice in London can be contacted on 020 7947 6564 or at the enquiry desk.

Lord Neuberger of Abbotsbury, Master of the Rolls
Sir Nicholas Wall, President of the Family Division
12 July 2010

APPENDIX B
APPLICATION FORM: NOTICE
OF MCKENZIE FRIEND

To be completed by the Applicant/Claimant or the Respondent/ Defendant

[Please fill in the form, take it to the court and hand it to the court usher **before the hearing starts.**]

Case Number:..

Parties: Applicant/Claimant...……..
          Respondent/Defendant:.......................................

I am the **Applicant/Claimant** ( ) / **Respondent/Defendant** ( )
(please tick)

I wish to have a McKenzie Friend with me at the hearing. I understand that my McKenzie Friend:-
1) may provide moral support; take notes; help with case papers; quietly give advice.
2) may not address the court, make oral submissions or examine witnesses unless the Judge gives permission;
3) in family matters, should not have an interest in the outcome of the proceedings.

<u>The McKenzie Friend</u> is (please tick)
(a) a relative (please give relationship) ......
(b) a friend/ neighbour/ colleague/ other (please specify) ....
(c) a free- advice agency worker ....
(d) a person I am paying to help in this case ....

If you have ticked box (c) or (d) above, please say what agency or organisation or association the person belongs to (if any).........

Name and Address of McKenzie Friend:

....

....

(business address if (c) or (d) above has been ticked)

The McKenzie Friend must complete below:-

1. Have you read the Practice Guidance issued on 12 July 2010 by the Head of Civil Justice and the Head of Family Justice? It is available online and displayed here http://www.judiciary.gov.uk/Resources/JCO/Documents/Guidance/mckenzie-friends-practice-guidance-july-2010.pdf .   **Yes / No**

2. Do you agree to comply with it?   **Yes / No**

3. Do you have a legal qualification? **Yes / No**
     If yes, please specify.................

The Judge may ask you questions about the above statements to satisfy him/herself that your answers are accurate. Those questions may be renewed at any subsequent hearing.

Signature of Litigant ....
Date   ....

MORE BOOKS BY
LAW BRIEF PUBLISHING

A selection of our other titles available now:-

'Covid-19, Homeworking and the Law – The Essential Guide to Employment and GDPR Issues' by Forbes Solicitors
'Covid-19, Force Majeure and Frustration of Contracts – The Essential Guide' by Keith Markham
'Covid-19 and Criminal Law – The Essential Guide' by Ramya Nagesh
'Covid-19 and Family Law in England and Wales – The Essential Guide' by Safda Mahmood
'Covid-19 and the Implications for Planning Law – The Essential Guide' by Bob Mc Geady & Meyric Lewis
'Covid-19, Residential Property, Equity Release and Enfranchisement – The Essential Guide' by Paul Sams and Louise Uphill
'Covid-19, Brexit and the Law of Commercial Leases – The Essential Guide' by Mark Shelton
'Covid-19 and the Law Relating to Food in the UK and Republic of Ireland – The Essential Guide' by Ian Thomas
'A Practical Guide to the General Data Protection Regulation (GDPR) – 2nd Edition' by Keith Markham
'Ellis on Credit Hire – Sixth Edition' by Aidan Ellis & Tim Kevan
'A Practical Guide to Working with Litigants in Person and McKenzie Friends in Family Cases' by Stuart Barlow
'Protecting Unregistered Brands: A Practical Guide to the Law of Passing Off' by Lorna Brazell
'A Practical Guide to Secondary Liability and Joint Enterprise Post-Jogee' by Joanne Cecil & James Mehigan

'A Practical Guide to Financial Services Claims' by Chris Hegarty

'The Law of Houses in Multiple Occupation: A Practical Guide to HMO Proceedings' by Julian Hunt

'A Practical Guide to Unlawful Eviction and Harassment' by Stephanie Lovegrove

'A Practical Guide to Solicitor and Client Costs' by Robin Dunne

'Occupiers, Highways and Defective Premises Claims: A Practical Guide Post-Jackson – 2nd Edition' by Andrew Mckie

'A Practical Guide to Financial Ombudsman Service Claims' by Adam Temple & Robert Scrivenor

'A Practical Guide to Advising Schools on Employment Law' by Jonathan Holden

'A Practical Guide to Running Housing Disrepair and Cavity Wall Claims: 2nd Edition' by Andrew Mckie & Ian Skeate

'A Practical Guide to Holiday Sickness Claims – 2nd Edition' by Andrew Mckie & Ian Skeate

'Arguments and Tactics for Personal Injury and Clinical Negligence Claims' by Dorian Williams

'A Practical Guide to QOCS and Fundamental Dishonesty' by James Bentley

'A Practical Guide to Drone Law' by Rufus Ballaster, Andrew Firman, Eleanor Clot

'A Practical Guide to Compliance for Personal Injury Firms Working With Claims Management Companies' by Paul Bennett

'A Practical Guide to the Landlord and Tenant Act 1954: Commercial Tenancies' by Richard Hayes & David Sawtell

'A Practical Guide to Dog Law for Owners and Others' by Andrea Pitt

'RTA Allegations of Fraud in a Post-Jackson Era: The Handbook – 2nd Edition' by Andrew Mckie

'RTA Personal Injury Claims: A Practical Guide Post-Jackson' by Andrew Mckie

'On Experts: CPR35 for Lawyers and Experts' by David Boyle

'An Introduction to Personal Injury Law' by David Boyle

'A Practical Guide to Chronic Pain Claims' by Pankaj Madan
'A Practical Guide to Claims Arising from Fatal Accidents' by James Patience
'A Practical Guide to Subtle Brain Injury Claims' by Pankaj Madan

These books and more are available to order online direct from the publisher at www.lawbriefpublishing.com, where you can also read free sample chapters. For any queries, contact us on 0844 587 2383 or mail@lawbriefpublishing.com.

Our books are also usually in stock at www.amazon.co.uk with free next day delivery for Prime members, and at good legal bookshops such as Wildy & Sons.

We are regularly launching new books in our series of practical day-to-day practitioners' guides. Visit our website and join our free newsletter to be kept informed and to receive special offers, free chapters, etc.

You can also follow us on Twitter at www.twitter.com/lawbriefpub.

Printed in Great Britain
by Amazon

23389391R00064